The Mystical Boy

Poems
by

Martyn Hesford

Cover photo: the author

ISBN: 9798857014332

PublishNation

Martyn Hesford is a BAFTA-nominated screenplay writer, theatre playwright and poet. His film screenplays include FANTABULOSA!, starring Michael Sheen, and MRS LOWRY AND SON, starring Vanessa Redgrave and Timothy Spall. His theatre plays have been performed at the Hampstead Theatre and the Trafalgar Studios, London. THE MYSTICAL BOY is Martyn Hesford's third collection of poems. His previous poetry collections are LILAC WHITE and SNOW STAR.

Poems, fairytale, magical
and mystical spells.
Coming together to make a prayer.

A poet's inner journey.

The poems can be read one at a time
or as a whole.

*For
Keith Sumner*

1

my eyes saw things

my ears heard everything

they thought I was sleeping

but
my heart felt

all.

2

you will never know
who I am

you did not want
to know me

you wanted me

to be silent

you wanted

my eyes
to shine

for you

you wanted

to keep me

in your glass
vanity box

a jewel

there was a price to be paid
for your gift of life to me

the life
I cannot return on your terms
I cannot be your desired
perfection

I am a different
soul

I am you
in flesh and blood

I am the same
heart

but
I am not yours
to own

we shall forgive each other
one day I hope

no more blame

I know
there is

a holiness

somewhere
in me

given

from you

to me

I want to be
not owned

but found

let me go

let me live

mother.

3

here
in darkness

the starlight

flowers

grow

mysteriously.

4

did you
know

each child
born

has a price

did you
know

you were
born
to make
someone

happy

did you
know

all

is
slowly
taken
away

did you
know

all

is
stolen

did you
know

innocence

is
always
left behind

buried
in

a
garden

smothered
by them

those
that gave
you life

those that
say

we love you

most.

5

through
the night
leave him
let him be
do not
pick
him
up
leave him
do not
stroke
his hair
leave him
do not
whisper
soft
little
whispers
into
his delicate
tiny ears

leave
him

do not
kiss

him

ever
go
to him
and you
will
ruin
him

let him
cry
himself
to sleep

let
his cries
of
loneliness
turn into
fear

the fear
will dissipate
and turn
into
anger

anger
will
make him
strong

let him
wear
himself out

sobbing
teach him

brutality

the ways
of
the world

the world of men

let him
know
about
cruelty

loneliness

violence

fear

let him
know

all
there is
to know

go
to sleep

hush

go
to sleep

hush

go to sleep

hush

punch

away

stab

cut

into
the fear

pierce
the heart

and
one day

you will
love

like me

and cry

like me

forever

said

my father.

6

I hide

inside
the old wardrobe
of bat
and ball
teddy bears
wax dolls
hoops and skittles
skates
the pots
of coloured paints

here
the jet black

raven

peers

through
the stained glass window

watching

blink blink

bevelled

distorted

he sees
me

the
boy

trapped

left alone

here
all is

wicked

evil

charmed

the gates of once upon a time

open

wide

here
beware
the old woman

the man

in a wig

their hands

to grab and catch
you

pinch stroke

and poke

the bedroom door
is chained and locked

the wardrobe door
rattles

the squeaking of a mouse

the night owl hoots

all is
magic

nightmares

hauntings
here

through a keyhole

I see

the doctor half sleeps
holding his knife

the nurse sharpens
her scissors

nobody is safe
locked away
in the big old house

listen

somewhere

down the crooked staircase

a black cat
meows

this is

a grown ups
world

all
is hidden

locked away

forgotten

secrets

what did you do to me

back then

was it
only

a small
murder
this cut
this stab

the slicing

this splintering

the killing

of my

childhood.

7

I escape

inside
a silver egg

I sleep

I dream

I am protected

but
I can hear
the soft

cracking
coming

the little
fragmentations

they call madness.

8

nothing
is real

here

nothing l can
touch

all is

a closed eyes
dream

the star people
appear

here

the witches

the silver wolves

anything is
possible

have you been
here

did you ever visit

have you ever
stepped out

from

who you
think
you really are

and
seen

the other side
of yourself

the backwards
reflection

in the mirror

there are stories
to find

clouds to climb

if only
you could admit
there is something
more

a closed eyes
world

but

be warned

if you do
come here

oh please
be careful

beware
the nurse
the doctor
who tries
to stop
you

for they
will give you
the medication
of
silent sleep

in their eyes

to stay
here

is madness

they prefer you
to stay put

in
the mortal world

rather
than climb
the stepladder over the moon

to find

the light and the dark

the silver shadows

this floating
dust

that
some

call

magic.

9

said the raven

do you believe in fairies
do you believe in angels

do you believe in prayers or spells

magic is magic

come with me
close your eyes

see

yourself

the little boy

his tiny feet
in white shoes
hang

branches
scratch
his legs

little
blood drops

fall

like
natures red berries

it hurts

he screams

wings
hold him
tight

the feathers
filling his mouth

they taste
of dried mud

flying
away

out

of

the blue

into
the rolling grey

a nest

in a tree branch
awaits

soon
the little boy
will forget
his human
home

here
in the air

he is
reborn

the chosen one
the stolen one

twig leaf
crowned

oh hail

the ravens
first love

the bird prince

one day King.

10

eyes wide
open
lost
in fairyland

I breathe

roses
red

full
petals

they fall
out
of my mouth

I am lying
in the white

I am naked

I cannot speak

trapped
in natures spell

my protection

her thorns

growing

around my head

a crown

I am
rose petal
full

eyes wide

I breathe

I bleed

there are bees

buzzing

I hear them

their wings
are little

their bodies
soft

they sting

they sting.

11

I have feathers growing
from my shoulders

from my left to my right

beautifully

strangely

this is not
a deformity

oh no

they are
my

wings

soon
I will be able to

fly

into the dark
into the light

I will

find

angels

and dance.

12

inside
my head

I hear
the church bell

of memory

it might have been a hundred years ago

there is
whiteness

I'm flying towards
the house

her face

at the window

watching

waiting
for me

the pleasure
her smile

the moments
to come

in this room
the little burst
of sparks

stars

floating
up
the chimney

me and her

together

even now

forevermore

the memory

this visitation

feels

holy

tea
with my gran

the cake and scones
the jam and bread

we shared
each Sunday

this ritual

a holy
cup of tea

with

Jesus.

13

even at
this small age

I knew

instinctively

there was something

more

to see
to feel

to find

beyond

the railings
and
broken glass

beyond

the violence
of men

the anger

of women

a world within a world
here
this mystery

the invisible

this light

I come here
to find

again and again

all is
faith

all is
faith

heaven

unseen

yet

felt.

14

do you remember
said the raven

they forced you away
from the playing streets

marched you
through
iron gates

a serpent and a sword
its
heart
in
thorns
entwined

the world of school long pants
boys like men
with floppy hair

some
were giants

bell to bell
corridor to corridor
the halls of noise
you crawled

you
crept away from
their laughter
their pushes

their calling of names

the burning
of your
fairy
wings

each
new day
the beginning
all those growing up years
to come

you
wrapped up
your soul
in tissue paper

buried it

in a hole

ashamed
forgotten

there you
survived

hidden away
a blind boy

waiting
for light

a white rose

to grow.

15

there are
others

alone

in the
darkness

thousands
and
thousands

I watch

two young
girls

sat together
under the moon

naked

the stars touch their feet

one girl is crying

the other is wailing

the glass of tears is full

yesterday
with stolen
kisses

he felt

both

their breasts

and more

he talked
of

love

felt both their breasts
and more

tonight
their
golden prince

their christ

will not
come

innocence

is stolen
quietly

here
purity

has

gone

the church bell
is silent

the angels voice

is muted

in cobwebs.

16

inside

my panic

I cannot
remember

the dream

I am
left with
a feeling

the smothering

of
every

butterfly

insects
crawl

inside
my lungs

yet

I still
breathe

I breathe.

17

when did you
become

disappointed

with
the outside
world

did it happen

gently

slowly

was it
a surprise

was it
out of the blue

did it
come
and go

this feeling
the loss

did you forget
father christmas
first
fairyland

or God

was it the death of a goldfish.

18

there are birds
flying

inside my head

flapping
their wings

I can hear
them

I can feel
them

my bandage
keeps them

tight

inside

they cannot
escape
through my ears

can you
see them

their
shadows

their scratching
behind
my eyes

do they think
my hair
is their
nest

they are not singing

they are screaming

they are screeching.

19

there are tears

falling

thousands
and thousands

tears

like stars

falling

into the darkness

do you think God lives here

sometimes I do.

20

the first time we met

you looked into my eyes

your face in
coloured lights

that night
you held me in your arms

your eyes
revealed a secret

everything
I needed to know

love

at first sight.

21

tender

little
kisses

soft
kisses

the touch

of
a butterfly's
wing

I shiver

little
shivers

for you

I look
into you

all is
melted

into

red

there are burns
shaping

onto my skin

forming

blistering

hearts

into red

blood
red.

22

I love the red. the warmth of blood. alive. the
promise of the unseen. tomorrow. the fading of
this year. the kiss. the distant barking dog. a
golden firework that explodes in heaven. the
cascading stars. the glittering. the renewal. all is
here. in the heart.

born.

23

I bow my head
in reverence

this symbol
this magic

bringing
together

each hand

held together

in prayer

making

in
the mystery

you and me

together

the sacred

as

one.

24

to see
as the child
sees

in older age

is
to remember

the wonder

the raindrops

their sparkle

falling slowly

in fairyland.

25

we flew over
the churches
the houses
the river below
you
in a white robe
me
in a blue bow tie
the bees
did not
seem to mind
that in
our pockets
we had
taken
their honey
the swan
did not know
that I had
a white feather
in my hair
the birds
gave us
their bread

we
sat on
the white cloud

eating
our picnic

then
we fell

down
to earth

we fell down to earth
together

holding hands.

26

and
you said

in
the silence

there is a flame
burning

it is
hiding
in the corner
of the room

it is
silver

against
the blue

burning

bright

this holy light

it is strength

see

this light

is never snuffed out

it
is you.

27

do not fear
do not fear
me gone

one day
this could happen

you said

take hold of fear
take hold of fear

stick out
the child's tongue

and
make fear

laugh.

28

and
in
the garden

there is
blossom

falling

the white and the pink

the perfection

bursting

gently

falling

again
again
again

one day
this will end

but
not today

today

the earth

is blessed.

29

I will build you a palace
a palace made of glass

the glass will reveal
everything

the people will see everything

we will have nothing more
to hide

they will see
us

doing everything

eating
washing

loving

they will see
us

loving

day and night

we shall live
naked

like every
other

animal

no more pretence
no more lies

and
the people
will see

through

the glass walls

and
they will say

oh
don't they look
beautiful

don't they look
beautiful

loving

oh

I wish
we could be
like them

oh
I wish
we could

love

till
kingdom come

but
they can't

you see

they never will

they don't
know how

they don't know
how to forgive

you have
to forgive

you have
to forgive

everything

everyone

if you're
to

love

you have to forgive

I forgive
you

do you

forgive

me

and I said
yes.

30

and you said
awake
into whiteness

awake
into brightness

what do you see
in the sparkle

eyes
hands

leaves
clouds

legs
fingers

grass

mouth

what do you see

do you see

everything

do you see

the invisible

do you see

you

a spark

the light

you

in everything

at all.

31

are you weeping

still

are you spoiling the flowers

still

do you blame

the others

this world

still

do you remember

the beginning

still

do you remember

the wonder

the innocent

the love

still.

32

though
buried

under
silver leaves

inside

he sees through
each little gap

the mystical

reflects all back

here

to forgive

to grow in spirit

is

to play
with
miracles

can you see

the white on white
the bright on bright
are you in the shadow of the glare

can you see

the blazing

the searing sight

the wings on white

this
holy light.

33

and
I see you

the angel

in the sky

hovering
over the sun

and
there is no sound

just a quiet
soaring

gold petals fall

gold slips gently
over my eyes

and
I see

a boy on the hill

wearing a crown

walking
towards me

he looks into my eyes

holding out his hand

he says nothing

he holds my hand

and
the sun blinds me

and
in
the brightness

the whiteness
of a room

there is
a poet

sitting
at
a table

pen in hand
he is writing
a poem

a prayer.

34

and
in the whiteness

the brightness

the last thorn is placed
upon the crown

and
I hear

the poet

his poem

a prayer

oh

if
they ever knew

the beauty
of

who we really are

a breath
a sigh

a smile

the purity
the simplicity

to see

to be

here

in this
moment

the sacred

the eternal

a leaf becomes a forest
a whisper becomes a storm

a star becomes the sparkle
of your own little tear

there is a place
forgotten

there is a place
hidden

the invisible world
inside our own

here
all is
fairyland

here

all is
heaven

here

all is
found.

35

my eyes saw things

my ears heard everything

they thought I was sleeping

but
my heart felt

all.

Printed in Great Britain
by Amazon

28144604R00050